A TRUE STATE OF THE CASE OF THE COMMONWEALTH

by

MARCHAMONT NEDHAM

Published by *The Rota* at the University of Exeter
1978

© The Rota, 1978

ISBN : 0 904617 09 2

The Rota is an independent, academic society,
wholly supported by its subscribers.
Its sole purpose is the publication of facsimilies
of the Stuart era.

This is the nineteenth pamphlet published by *The Rota*.
For more information please contact
Maurice Goldsmith or Ivan Roots
at the University of Exeter.

Printed in Great Britain by
The Printing Unit of the University of Exeter

PREFATORY NOTE

A true state of the case of the commonwealth, dated by Thomason 9 February 1653/4, is an apology, probably official, for the arrangements of the Protectorate — a single person and a parliament (with a council) — recently instituted under the Instrument of Government (12 December 1653). It justified the series of events by which the Protectorate had (providentially) come into being. Parliament opposing the King, the Army's various interventions, Cromwell turning out the Rump and later dismissing the Nominated Assembly, none of these had been intended to result in a particular form of government, though all aimed to establish true religion and to protect English liberties. This genetic justification of the Protectorate was matched by a eulogy of its constitution, which under the Instrument wisely avoided the dangers of tyranny by placing the legislative and executive powers in different hands and eschewed the evil of continuous parliaments while setting up a succession of triennial meetings of at least five months' duration. 'If we take a survey of the whole together, we find the Foundation of this Government laid by the People' (p. 28) and 'the Liberties of England not only secured but enlarged' (p. 29). Official approval is evident from Cromwell's use of *A true state* in his speech of 12 September 1654 and his express commendation on 22 January 1654/5; see W. C. Abbott, *Writings and speeches of Oliver Cromwell* (Cambridge, Mass., 1937-47), III, 587.

Marchmont Nedham (1620-1678), who wrote for almost every party during the 1640s and 50s, was the author of *A true state*. It is attributed to him by Abbott (III, 193) and by C. H. Firth, *The last years of the Protectorate* (London, 1909), I, 156, presumably on the grounds of style and content; in addition Blair Worden has identified a passage (p. 10) taken from his *Mercurius politicus* (1-8 July 1652), pp. 1705-6; see *The Rump Parliament* (Cambridge, 1974), p. 362.

Born at Burford, Oxfordshire, Nedham went up at fourteen to All Souls as a chorister. Soon after taking his B.A. in 1637, he became an usher at Merchant Taylors' and then underclerk at Gray's Inn (admitted in 1652). He wrote much of *Mercurius Britanicus* (first issue, 16-22 August 1642), which was established by Parliament to counter the influential royalist newsheet, *Mercurius aulicus*. His witty but galling style eventually got him into trouble: a violent attack on the King put him in gaol. In 1646 he was again imprisoned; bailed , he was forbidden to publish because he commented on the sensitive relation between the Houses of Parliament. From his retreat to the practice of medicine, he emerged with a contribution to the *Gangraena* controversy, *Independencie no schisme* (16 July 1646). In *The case of the kingdom stated* (12 June 1647) and *The lawyer of Lincolnes-Inn reformed* (1 July 1647), Nedham advocated an alliance between the Independents and the King. He is said to have submitted personally to the King and in September began writing *Mercurius pragmaticus*. Although captured and gaoled in June 1649, he was released in November. Within a year he had turned Commonwealth propagandist, being voted fifty pounds for writing *The case of the Commonealth of England, stated* (8 May 1650; ed. P. A. Knachel; Charlottesville, Va., 1969) and one hundred pounds a year for undertaking *Mercurius politicus* in which he repeated the arguments of *The case of the Commonwealth*. John Milton, Nedham's nominal superior, is sometimes credited with influencing him at this time. Nedham also edited *The Publick intelligencer*, but *Mercurius politicus* was the principal outlet for his views, many of which he later republished in *The excellencie of a free-state* (1656). He managed to tack to, even indeed anticipate, the shifting winds of Commonwealth politics, but having written against a restoration in 1659 (*Interest will not lie* and *News from Brussels*), he fled in 1660 to Holland. Somehow he procured a pardon and returned to practice medicine — publishing on that subject and on education until being recalled to political journalism by Charles II with *A pacquet of advices and animadversions sent from London to the men of Shaftesbury* (1676) and other tracts. For accounts of Nedham's career, see C. H. Firth in *D.N.B.* and J. Frank, *The beginnings of the English newspaper, 1620-1660* (Cambridge, Mass., 1961).

Nedham's writings are notable for their tongue-in-cheek manner, which he himself referred to as 'drolling'; see *Mercurius politicus* 352 (5-12 March 1657), pp. 7641-44. His views show the influence of Machiavelli's republicanism and frequently attempt a cool analysis of the 'interests' of the political actors involved. Discussions of his views may be found in P. Zagorin, *A history of political thought in the English revolution* (London, 1954), pp. 121-27 and J. A. W. Gunn, *Politics and the public interest in the seventeenth century* (London, 1969), pp. 33-35, 43-44, 48, 51-53.

A true state of the case of the commonwealth, Wing T3114, is reproduced with the permission of the Board of the British Library; shelf mark E. 728 (5). *The Rota* is grateful to Professor A. H. Woolrych for help with this note.

A TRUE
State of the Case

OF THE

COMMONVVEALTH

OF

England, *Scotland*, and *Ireland*,

And the Dominions thereto belonging;

In reference to the late established Government

BY A

Lord Protector,

and a *PARLAMENT*.

Manifesting therein, not only a Consistencie with, and necessary Consequence upon the foregoing Alterations; but also a full Conformity to the declared Principles and Engagements of the *Parlament* and *Army*.

It being the Judgment of divers Persons, who, throughout these late Troubles, have approved themselves faithfull to the Cause and Interest of GOD and their Country.

Presented to the Publick, for the satisfaction of others.

London, Printed by *Tho. Newcomb*, over against *Baynards-Castle* in *Thames-street.* 1654. 1653

A TRUE
STATE of the CASE
OF THE
Common-wealth,
In reference
To the late eſtabliſh'd *Government*
BY A
Ld PROTECTOR
and a *PARLAMENT.*

Eeing it hath pleaſed GOD, after many various and wonderfull Turns of Affairs, (occaſioned through the continual oppoſitions of his, and his Peoples enemies on the one ſide, banding themſelves againſt the Rights and Liberties of this Nation ; and on the other ſide, through the Corruption and Apoſtaſie of particular Perſons, who have from time to time been intruſted in the Supreme Authority) at length to fix the Government of theſe Dominions in the preſent Form of Eſtabliſhment : As it is a matter much beyond the expectation of thoſe whom He hath uſed as Inſtruments in the whole courſe

of

of his Providence, and of admiration to the World; so it affords abundant cause of praise and thankfgiving ; that thofe great Changes and Revolutions which have been in the midft of us, have not engaged us in blood among our felves, nor expofed us for a prey and fpoil to the Common Enemy, who watcheth all advantages and opportunities to promote the ruine of that Intereft, which the Lord himfelf hath owned by many glorious Deliverances in the behalf of our Nation : for no other Reafon can be imagined of the happy peace and tranquillity which we now enjoy, but that He who ftretched out the Heavens, and laid the foundations of the Earth, and formeth the fpirit of Man within him, hath brought forth thefe things, as the accomplifhment of his own good will and purpofe toward his People ; who have been carried on by a Divine hand, through many admirable difficulties and fucceffes, in all the contefts they have had with the Enemies of their Peace and Liberty.

And as fuch Difpenfations as thefe cannot be lookt upon, by the moft envious eye or profane heart, as the birth and product of any fore-laid Contrivements of men, biaffed with corrupt and carnal intereft ; So we have a great ground of hope and confidence, that the Lord, in whofe hands is our breath and life, and all our wayes, hath been fhaking and moving foundations in thefe Lands, not to overturn, but to eftablifh this Commonwealth upon a better and more fure *Bafis* of Government, than hath been enjoyed by our Anceftors for many Generations. And truly, we cannot but profefs our felves very much raifed with hopes and apprehenfions of this nature, as often as we refled upon the Refolutions lately taken for the fettlement of thefe Nations, and expofed in Print to the view of the World : which doubtlefs being confidered in themfelves, and compared with the beft of former Governments, do not only exceed the wifhes and expedations of thofe men, who caft an eye of prejudice upon all the Adions and Proceedings of the prefent Governours, and are fory to fee perfons whom they hate and maligne, become Inftruments of any good ;

but

but we conceive also, that being weighed in an equal ballance
they do in substance, and upon a true account, fully corre-
spond with the primary Ends and Intentions of such as engaged in the late Controversie with the King , upon principles of common Freedom, and have not since been drawn
aside through the subtilties of Satan (leading them captive
by a deluded phansie) to promote the things they have not
seen ; or not designed peculiar advantages of their own
some other way, and calculated their particular Interests for
another kind of Government : From neither of which any
great compliance with the present can be expected, untill
the one Party awake out of their dreams of an imaginary
Paradise , and the other find a door open'd again to their
private Interest and advantage. And therefore, though we
apprehend it would be time ill spent, to endeavour the re-
ducing of such men by dint of Reason and Argument ;
yet in regard divers Doubts may seem to arise in the minds
of some sober men concerning the present Change, (especi-
ally now when the Age abounds with calumny , and our
Enemies make it their business by cunning insinuations to
draw away the hearts of the Well-affected from their best
Friends ;) as if we had turned our backs upon our former
Principles, and introduced again that very Thing, which was
the great Bone of contention, (the removal whereof seemed
to include the very state of the Quarrel between the late
King and the Parliament) and so fought our selves round
till we rest upon the old bottom , and in conclusion given
judgment against our selves in all the things contended for
against the King ; hereupon we have thought meet, in all
meeknefs and moderation, to present our Judgment to the
publike view, and offer such Particulars to others , as may
(through the blessing of God) be a ground of satisfaction
to them, as well as to our selves ; being fully perswaded in
our own breasts, as to the present Form of Government,
that such Cautions and Limitations are therein described ; as
make due and full provision for the Peoples Liberties , and
those just Rights, the maintenance whereof hath been so
reti-

(4)

religiously profecuted in the late War; and that it contains nothing contrary to, or inconfiftent with thofe good purpofes and principles, held forth by the Parliament and Army in their feveral Declarations; but is clearly juftifiable both by them and by right Reafon, according to the practifes and proceedings hitherto owned by the Parliament themfelves, the Army, and all the well-affected party, in feveral alterations upon the like occafions of neceffity.

Now in order to the clearing of thefe things, we conceive it requifite, firft, to confider, what was the original Ground of our taking Arms, and upon what Foot that Quarrel ftood: And then in the fecond place, How it came to pafs that the Army were conftrained divers times to declare and interpofe themfelves after an extraordinary manner, in profecuting our firft principles, through the many great changes of Affairs and revolutions of Government; touching which we fhall not here take upon us to difpute by inches, the occafions of our Change into a Free-State or Commonwealth, and the feveral Tendencies thereunto; nor fhall we run over all thofe Particulars in Difcourfe at large, feeing they are matters well known to the godly People of this Nation (whofe fatisfaction we principally intend) and have heretofore been declared at full; but we fhall content our felves only with a fummary repetition of the main Particulars, fo far as is neceffary to evince the equity of their then-Proceeding, and give light to clear the way of our following Difcourfe; in all which we doubt not but it will manifeftly appear, that they were concerned out of confcience and duty, to acquit themfelves as they did; unlefs they would have ftood ftill, as idle fpectators or Parties unconcerned, while men of loofe or debauched principles and corrupt minds, were perfidioufly contriving the publick ruine, contracting new Interefts and Parties contrary to the old, and abfolutely deftructive to all the primitive points infifted upon.

I. And

I. And first, as concerning the original ground of our first engaging in the War, We shall take leave to premise this one Thing for an unquestionable Truth; That we never fought, nor was it ever declared by the Parliament or Army, that we took up Arms for, or against any particular Form of Government whatsoever. Look over all the Declarations, Remonstrances, and Protestations made by either, and it will appear that we never fought against the King, as King; nor for the Parliament or Representative consider'd purely as such: But we took up Arms against the King because he demeaned himself as a Tyrant, and had projected a wicked design of introducing his own Will and Power above Law; and for the Parliament or Representative, because it seemed to be the likeliest and best means (as Affairs then stood) to prevent those manifold evils which threatned the Kingdom, and to preserve the Liberties of the People. And therefore (we say) Government under this or that Form, was not the moving Cause of this great Controversie, but those common ends of safety and Freedom, for which all sorts of Governments were instituted and appointed. Yea, and it must here be remember'd, that even at that time, when the Army put forth that Remonstrance from St. *Albans*, which usher'd in the King to the Bar of Justice, they had not then entertained any thoughts of excluding Government by Kings, provided they were *Elective*. And as for the King himself, there appeared not the least intentions to cast him off, till he had quite cast off the People, and would admit no reconciliation but upon his own Terms, such as must necessarily have frustrated those righteous ends of our first Engaging. Moreover, whosoever shall take a serious view of all the Papers that have been made publick, to set forth the Grounds of the War, shall ever find, that the main Point insisted on by the Parliament and Army in their many Declarations, was, *The bringing Delinquents to condign punishment, the maintenance of the Laws and Liberties of the Land, and of a due succession of Parliaments.* **This was the Soul**

Soul that animated their whole Undertaking; which was not by them intended to quarrel at the Kingly Form then eſtabliſhed, but to regulate the diſorders and exceſſes of the King and his Government, and reduce him within the due bounds of Authority; that he might not accompliſh that deſigne which had been the buſineſs of his whole Reign, *viz.* the advancement of his own and his Poſterities Will and Power, againſt the publick Intereſt of the Nation. Hence it was, that his legal Intereſt was ſtill admitted in all Declarations, and his juſt Power and greatneſs provided for in them, and in the *Covenant*; but with this remarkable reſtriction or ſpecial Limitation, [*In the preſervation of the true Religion and Liberties of the Kingdoms;*] and the ſaid Declarations ſtill directed us to the equitable ſenſe of all Laws and Conſtitutions, as diſpenſing with the very Letter of the ſame, and being ſupreme to it, when the ſafety of all is concerned.

I I. And therefore in the ſecond place, that it may plainly appear, what juſt cauſe both the Parliament and Army had to recede from the Letter of their former Profeſſions toward the Kings Perſon and Family, and how they were (through his default) neceſſitated to give way to the ſubſequent Alterations, we ſhall only in general terms ſet down a brief Account of Things in reference to that great buſines, and to the ſeveral changes that have followed ſince, out of which the neceſſity and Juſtneſs of the preſent Change wil in ſome meaſure appear.

When after the expence of much precious bloud, and many Treaties to no purpoſe, it was clearly found by experience, that the King was obſtinately and irrecoverably engaged in the proſecution of ſuch Courſes as portended nothing but ſpeedy ruine to the Kingdome; and rendred him utterly irreconcileable to the Parliament in their juſt Addreſſes and demands; ſo that there was no poſſibility of a ſettlement by him, in any way that might anſwer the Truſt repoſed in them by their Country. And in
regard

regard there was a Corrupt Party prevailing afterward in Parliament, who had declined the true declared Interest, and designed to re-invest him with the exercise of Kingly Power, without any competent Security, or reasonable Provision for the declared Rights and Liberties of the People, or for those that had faithfully engaged in the maintenance of them : These things being considered, with the calamities and desolations inevitably drawing on, unless some immediate and extraordinary remedy were found to obviate the design; it pleased God at length to excite such as remained faithful both in Parliament and Army, by a seasonable Interposition to give a stop to these mens Intentions; And seeing it was impossible to secure the Interest of Religion and Liberty, with respect had any longer to the King himself, he was utterly laid aside; the Consideration of those great Ends being superior to the dignity of his Person.

Now, as this first most remarkable Alteration in the Parliamentary Affairs, was not only just and honourable in it self, but esteemed so, and therefore avowed by the honest and well-affected of the Nation, and necessitated by the inconstancie of that Party of men in Parliament, who (contrary to their trust) would have yielded up the precious Concernments of the People as to Religion and Liberty, together with the Parliament it self, unto the meer will and power of the King ; (yea, and this when he had stood it out to the last, and was within the power of the Army:) So also, when after his necessary Imprisonment, in order to the security and peace of the Nation, it was observed, that though he had alter'd his condition, he retained his old obstinate mind and resolution ; and it appeared moreover by experience, what an Influence he stil held upon the Parliament as then constituted ; insomuch that being encouraged by Insurrections and Commotions in all Parts of the Kingdom, they designed to bring him in upon a Treaty : And though in the Terms of that Treaty very little respect was had to the just ends of the Quarrel,

B   and

and the Prince, his Son, then in the revolted Ships at Sea,
disavowed all that should be done, and declared his Father
as a Prisoner in no condition to Treat ; yet so loft and loose
were that Party of men to all former Principles, that his re-
stauration was in a manner concluded , and oportunity e-
nough intended him to break all Bonds of Agreement, and
re-settle himself in an absolute arbitrary power , over the
Consciences and Liberties of the People. All which being laid together, as also, that the bloudy imbroilments in
the year 1648. and the Invasion of *Hamilton* , were to be
put upon his Account ; that by this means he had involved
himself and Family afresh in the guilt of Bloud ; and that
both He, and his Wife and Children , had for ever espoused
an Interest of their own , destructive to the Rights of the
Kingdom; then the Affairs of the Nation being driven to
the utmost Point of necessity, the Parliament were (in prudence) to look no farther for satisfaction , as formerly, in
the way of demanding our Rights ; but concerned (in conscience) to think of satisfying Divine Justice , by offering
him up a Sacrifice for the crie of innocent bloud, and after-
wards to take care for an establishment some other way , for
the safety and Freedom of our Nation : And therefore in
those after-actings toward the next great Alteration, when
they exterminated his Family and altered the Government,
they were every way to be justified in point of Conscience
and Prudence (notwithstanding former Declarations) for as
much as a Kingly Family and Office are but of a secondary
consideration to the security of a Kingdom , and all Forms
of Civil administration (being as the Shell to the Kernell)
are subordinate and inferior to the ends of Government; so
that if these cannot otherwise be attained , there follows
an unavoidable necessity of altering the Form.

The Government then of this Nation being(through necessity) alter'd , and at length established in the way of a
Free-State or Commonwealth in the hands of the Parliament, both the Army and People were content to acquiesce
therein,

(9)

therein, and continued languifhing year after year, in hope
at laft to have tafted thofe Fruits of Freedom, which feemed to fhoot forth and flourifh in the Bud, at the beginning
of that Eftablifhment : But when after the intercurrence of
divers years, all our hopes were blafted, in regard particular Members became ftudious of Parties and private Interefts, neglecting the publick; and by reafon of their dila-
tory Proceedings in the Houfe, and unlimited arbitrary
decifions at Committees, wholly perverted the end of
Parliaments; fo that the People being delaied (and fo in
effect denied)Anfwers to their Petitions,no dore being open
for the redrefs of Grievances, nor any hope of eafing the
People of their burthens, it was found at length by experience,that a ftanding Parliament was it felf the greateft Grievance; which appeared yet the more exceedingly grievous,
in regard of a vifible defigne carried on by fome among
them, to have perpetuated the Power in their own Hands,
infomuch that they never made any the leaft fhew of a new
Reprefentative or Parliament, till they underftood that the
Army were refolved to end their fitting. Then it was,
and not before, that they brought on their *Bill for a new
Reprefentative*; and this meerly out of defigne too, that
they might have had fome fhadow of Pretext to thwart or
fcandalize that moft neceffary work of Diffolution by the
Army. But notwithftanding admit, that they had been
real in their Intentions, for the putting a period to their
own Authority (as was pretended) and giving way to a fuc-
ceffion by the promoting of that *Bill*; yet confidering the
very Form of Succeffive Parliaments defcribed therein, in-
tending that the Supreme Authority fhould be lodged in
Biennial Parliaments, and that they fhould have power to
fit to make Laws, and Govern from two years to two years
fucceffively (keeping by that means the Supreme Legiflative Power alwayes in being) the evil confequences thereof
both in refpect of freedom and fafety,are difcernable to every eye, and would have proved a remedy worfe than the
difeafe.For befides the infinite number of Laws which would
B 2   have

have bin Enacted by the conſtant ſitting of the ſupreme Authority, that in a few years no man could have told how to
have behaved himſelf, either in reſpect of his life or eſtate,
(as is known by experience of the laſt Parliament , who
made more Laws then had been in ſome hundreds of years
before) the Supreme Powers of making Laws, and of putting them in execution , were by that Bill to have been di-
ſpoſed in the ſame hands; which placing the *Legiſlative* and
executive Powers in the ſame perſons , is a marvellous In-let
of Corruption and Tyranny : whereas the keeping of
theſe two apart , flowing in diſtinct Channels , ſo that they
may never meet in one (ſave upon ſome tranſitory extraordinary occaſion) there lies a grand Secret of Liberty and
good Government : And though it be of a dangerous im-
port , that they ſhould both reſt in the hands of any ſingle
perſon , excluding the Community ; yet the conſequents
are abundantly more pernicious , when they are graſped by
many : becauſe as a particular perſon is eaſily noted for his
exceſſes ; ſo particular offenders find ſhelter in a Multitude,
when whatſoever they Act , uſually paſſeth in the name of
the whole Body ; by which means, in effect, they become
unaccountable for Abuſes in Government. And how eaſily ſuch Abuſes might have been juſtified in a Parliamentary way, is apparent enough ; ſeeing an oportunity was given in that Bill, to the next , or any ſucceeding Parliament
(no manner of balance or Check being reſerved upon them)
by claiming an abſolute Authority to be in themſelves , for
ever to have continued the Power (if they pleaſed) in their
own hands , upon pretentions of ſafety ; by which means
the People muſt either wholly have loſt their Liberty , or
been involved again in Bloud, to remove the one , and re-
deem the other ; for, it is very evident , how prone men in
Power are to keep up themſelves , even from the carriage of
the late Parliament, which, had it been left to it ſelf, would
unqueſtionably have ſate for ever. And therefore it was
the wiſdom and care of our Anceſtors, ſo to temper the Government of our Nation in time paſt, that they left the Supreme

preme *Law-making Power* among the People in Parliament, to fit at fome times, and be-trufted the *Execution of Law*, with the myfteries of Government, in the hands of a fingle perfon and his Council. But the Leaders of the Parliament, fteering another Courfe in their *Biennial Bill*, did fet open a wide dore to the aforefaid Inconveniences, in that ominous Scheme of Government by them propounded. And thereby, as alfo by their own mifcarriages, made it manifeft to the judgments of the moft fober and well-affected People, that nothing of fettlement or fatiffaction could be expected from them, in order to the remedy of growing evils and neceffities, or to the prefervation of the chief ends of the late War. And in truth, it being utterly impoffible in that corrupted State, through long continuance in an unaccountable condition of Authority, that they who made it the main of their bufinefs to exercife an arbitrary power in Committees, and promote parties and Factions among Themfelves, and were like in a fhort time to overwhelm the ancient Liberties and Properties of the People, and increafe their vexations, through the multitude of unneceffary Laws (many of which were made upon occafion of, and to ferve and fuit with the Concernments and Interefts of particular Members) fhould become the Inftruments of our long-defired eftablifhment; And feeing no regard was had to the many humble follicitations of the Army, applyed to the moft confiderable Members of the Houfe, that others might fucceed in their Places, to perfect that good work which we had with fo much patience expected; therefore it became an Act no lefs pious then neceffary, for the Army to interpofe upon the fame equitable grounds as heretofore, in like cafes of extremity, and (no ordinary *medium* being left) to provide for the Main, in a way irregular and extraordinary, by a timely Diffolution; the confideration of the faid ends of our Engagement, and of Government it felf, being equally paramount to the priviledges of Parliament, as to the Prerogatives and Perfons of Kings.

And

And now the Army having proceeded thus far in that unaccuftomed (yet moft neceffary) way of action, not without much regret and hazard to themfelves ; whereas ill-minded men have taken occafion thereupon to blaft the fincerity of that Act , as if it had been an unworthy confequence of fome long fore-laid Defign upon grounds of Policie ; there needs (we fuppofe) no other coufuration of that calumny, then a bare confideration of the irrefolution and unpreparednefs of the Army at that time, as to any particular way of Settlement. For, although the Army (out of the fenfe they had of the evils hanging over our heads, and which were like to increafe while the Parliament fate)had taken fome confideration how to remedy the fame, and had before had conference about it with feveral Members of Parliament ; yet untill they were actually diffolved, no Refolutions were taken in what Model to caft the Government; but it was after the faid diffolution debated and difcuffed by the Officers of the Army, as *res integra* ; the Queftion being then put, Whether the Power fhould be referved in the hands of a few, or of a greater number of perfons, in order to an Eftablifhment : It was cohceived by fome, that the former would prove the more effectual Mean ; but by others, that the latter would be every jot as effectual, and befides bring this advantage along with it, that it would be much more fatisfactory to the generality of the Army , and to the good people of the Nation : whereupon, the Officers being defirous (as much as in them lay) to promote a Succeffion of Supreme Affemblies, in that form of a Free-State or Commonwealth which had been declared by Parliament, it was at length refolved to fall upon the latter, as being fuppofed the moft rational way (confidering all circumftances attending the conftitution of affairs) to provide for the eafe and fatisfaction of the people : And in order hereunto, it was agreed likewife, that fuch perfons fhould be called together out of the feveral Counties, as were reputed men fearing God, and of approved

proved fidelity; in the choice of which perſons ſuch in-
differencie was uſed, and ſo equal liberty allowed to all
then preſent with the *Generall*, that every Officer enjoyed
the ſame freedom of nomination, and the majority of ſuf-
frage carried it for the election of each ſingle Member:
By which means the ſupreme Power of the Nation was devolved and be-truſted into the hands of thoſe men thus elected, to all intents and purpoſes.

And truly, the hopes conceived, and expectations raiſed
from the meeting of that Aſſembly, were neither few, nor
without ground; foraſmuch as it was apprehended, the
perſons generally were men of godlineſs and honeſty, and
ſuppoſed to have a ſpirit as large as the Intereſt of Gods
people, (and ſurely many ſuch there were among them)
which Intereſt is doubtleſs of ſuch a latitude, that all men
who have the evidence of Regeneration, of faith, and love,
(though under different Forms, or not perſwaded yet
what Forms they ought to ſubmit unto, by reaſon of the
various diſputes about them) and do neither apoſtatize
from Forms and deride them, nor reject Chriſt in the
Communion of Saints, nor ſlight the holy Scriptures,
(which practiſes are altogether inconſiſtent with Godlineſs)
ſhould poſſeſs their Rights in an equal enjoyment of protection and liberty; And alſo, that men as men (notwith-
ſtanding the ſigns of Regeneration appear not in them)
ſhould enjoy the benefit of their reſpective Intereſts, whether in Articles of War, or any other Claims of a Civil
cogniſance. But on the contrary, it ſo fell out in a ſhort
time, that there appeared many in this Aſſembly of very
contrary principles to the Intereſt aforeſaid; which led
them violently on to attempt and promote many things,
the conſequence whereof(however it might not be intended
by the generality of them) would have been *A ſubverting
the Fundamental Laws of the Land, the deſtruction of Propriety, and an utter extinguiſhing the Miniſtry of the Goſpel.*
In truth, their principles led them to a pulling down all,
and eſtabliſhing nothing: So that inſtead of the expected

Settlement, they were running out into meer Anarchy and confusion.

For the further clearing whereof, it will be convenient here to give a short Systeme of their Principles and
actings, in reference, 1.to *Religion*, 2. to the *Civil Rights*
and *Laws* of the Nation. 3. to the *Army*; And though
we take little pleasure in a discourse of this nature, which
tends to a laying open the weaknefs and Failings of our
Brethren;yet feeing it is for their fakes that we doe it,who
in popular diforders and confufions, will have the greateft fhare of mifery and oppreffion;. We conceive it very
neceffary to fpeak our knowledg therein, and fhall proceed
with all tendernefs in the Relation, with intent (not to
afperfe any, but) only to fhew how farr the Members
Themfelves were concerned in confcience and duty, to refolve upon the diffolution of that Affembly.

And firft, as to *Religion*, We muft here (with grief of
heart) remember; how often the Profeffion of it, the
Ordinances, and the very name of Chrift was blafphem-
ed, by faftening a mark of Antichriftianifm upon every
thing they liked not; what fevere Principles of *Impofition*
were owned by thofe very men, who had fo often heretofore declaimed againft it, as that which had been an occafion of fpilling the Bloud of many Thoufands of precious Saints, and would again (under ftranger Pretences)
in a fhort time, have introduced a new Fury of Perfecu-
tion more high than ever; and by decrying all other
waies to eftablifh their own, have impofed a more than
Antichriftian Yoak upon the necks of Believers. Hence
it was, that they un-fainted every man, whofe Confcience
was not of the fame fize with their own, and condemned
all as Enemies to Reformation, who kept not an even pace
with Themfelves in the Houfe, or with the hot men at
BlackFryers Meeting, who pronounced all the Reformed Churches to be as the Out-works to *Babylon*, and that
they muft be taken down before there could be a coming
at

at the main Fort. Thus they became Judges over their Brethren, branding them as men of carnal and of Antichristian spirits, opposers of the work of God, &c. because not of the same perswasion in the Things held forth by them, though little was said to convince those that were contrary-minded : Nevertheless, they proceeded so far, as to make this the Foundation of a Breach in the House, among persons of the same Faith, and under a high name for Religion; by which means themselves became the great obstructors of the work of Reformation and Settlement. And now if these things had been managed by them in a fair seeming course of Reason and Argument, there might (perhaps) have been a way open'd to give or receive satisfaction ; but alas, that *Imposing spirit* of theirs was actuated, by a more high and active spirit of Dreams and Phantasie, which set an end to reasoning, and led them out to a pretence of infallibility in all their determinations; and what Influence this would have had in time upon mens Estates and Properties, is easily apprehended; seeing such a spirit as knows neither Bond nor Bound in things rational and civil, would soon have urged their arbitrary Dictates and Decisions for Law, as well as Gospel. Upon this account it was, that they and their followers presumed also, to declare the whole Ministry of the Nation *Antichristian*, and because those in Power did not readily concur with them in the same opinion, they branded both the Governors and Government, as *Babylonish* and Antichristian; upon which supposition only (without reasoning the matter) they would have pulled down the Ministry, both root and branch ; and their Party abroad in Pulpits, uttered many peremptory predictions of the remove or downfall, both of the one and the other. And whereas it was conceived necessary by many of the House, that all satisfaction should be given to the godly of the Nation, in reference to a Reformation of the Ministry, by ejecting such as were scandalous, at length an Expedient was thought of, and brought in from a Committee by way

C

of

of Report ; that Commiffioners fhould be fent into each County , with power to enquire into the lives and Doctrines of Minifters, and remove fuch as were offenfive, or fcandalous to their holy Profeffion: yet when the Queftion was put, it paffed in the *Negative* ; nothing would fatisfie but the Minifters muft down , and be turned out of all (both good and bad) to feek a fubfiftence for Themfelves and their Families; which had been not only a manifeft invafion of their Rights, as civil men, and Members of the Commonwealth , and a grievous Intrenchment upon the liberty of their Confciences , and of thofe who have been co werted by their Miniftry ; but feeing alfo, that many, at the fame inftant when they preffed this extirpation, profeffed fully againft the Magiftrates power in any matters of Religion, and particularly that of placing or fending forth men to Preach the Gofpel , we cannot underftand what hope there could be, of ever having a conftant Preaching Miniftry re-fetled in this Nation. And yet all the while, thefe men would have the world believe, that they are for a Godly Miniftry, for Liberty of Confcience, and that they abhor impofing upon their brethren. But by thefe things you may fee, what the confequents of their Principles would be touching Religion.

II. As to the *Laws* and *Civil Rights* of the Nation; When the point of Law came into confideration in the Houfe, the one Party was for pruning away its exuberances and fuperfluities; the other, for a hewing down of the main Body : The more fober Judgments were for a regulation of the Law, by making it more fuccinct, intelligible, and certain, as alfo to remedy the Abufes of it, and render it lefs tedious and chargeable to the People ; yet nothing would ferve the other , but a total eradication of the old, and introduction of a new : And fo the good old Laws of *England* (the Guardians of our lives and Fortunes) eftablifhed with prudence , and confirmed by the experience of many ages and generations (the prefervati-

on

on whereof was a principal Ground of our late Quarrel with the King) having been once abolished, what could we have expected afterward, but an inthroning of arbitrary Power in the Seats of Judicature, and an exposing of our Lives, our Estates, our Liberties, and all that is dear unto us, as a Sacrifice to the boundless appetite of meer Will and Pleasure. For, it hath been said of old; *The Law is that which puts a difference betwixt Good and Evil, betwixt Just and Unjust : If you once take away the Law, all things will fall into a confusion; every man will become a Law unto himself, which in the depraved condition of Humane Nature must needs produce many great Enormities : Lust will become a Law, and Envy will become a Law, Covetousness and Ambition will become Laws; and what Dictates, what Decisions such Laws will produce, may easily be discerned.* As for our parts, we in this Nation may easily perceive the event of such courses, having lived some years at the pleasure of a long-continued Parlament, who contrary to their Trust, and the nature of a Parlament (whose great work is to make Laws) took upon them ordinarily to administer Law and Justice, according to their own wills, and endeavoured to perpetuate the Office of Administration in their own hands, against the will of the People : In which Acts of absolute and Lordly power, as they were followed to the heels by this last Assembly; so these exceeded them in other dangerous attempts, which extended not only to the abolition of Law, but to the utter subversion of Civill right and Propriety. For, there was a Party of men among them, who assumed to themselves only the name of Saints; from which Title they excluded all others that were not of their Judgment and opinion, and therefore seeing it is a name that shall be had in everlasting honour; we are heartily sorry to have seen it so wretchedly abused in this Age of light and godliness, as that the pretence of it hath by some men been intended for a Rise to the advantages of worldly Power and glory, above the rest of their brethren.

For,

For what elfe could be the intention of thofe in the laft
Houfe ? who were no fooner met, but they would have
waved the way of Call upon a humane account, and generally made pretence to an extraordinary Call from *Chrift*
himfelf, and to take upon them to rule the Nation by vertue of a fuppofed Right of Saintfhip in themfelves ; and
upon this principle would have laid the foundation of a
new platform , which was to go under the name of a
Fifth Monarchy, never to have an end, but to war with
all other Powers, and break them in peeces. In order
whereunto , that they might make way for this *Fifth
Kingdom*, they and their party having wrefted and fitted
Scriptures for their turn, profeffed and declared abroad
(and into this princip'e and perfwafion they baptized all
their Profelytes) that the Powers in being were all branch-
es of the *Fourth Monarchy*, which muft be rooted up and
deftroyed : whereupon they took the confidence not
only to afperfe and judge whole States and Governments,
and prophefie their ruine, but did, as much as in them lay,
devove them to deftruction,and thereby prepare the fpirits
of the people to imbrace any opportunity to follow them
and put their defigns in execution. So that if their defign
of fetting up the *Fifth Monarchy* according to the dreams
they had of it, had taken effect, wherein men could have
had no other Right but what they muft have derived from
them and their Party ; it is no hard matter to difcern how
the common Intereft of this Nation would have been
fwallowed up by a particular Faction, and what a pernicious Engine it muft have proved to the perverting of all
Order among Men ; forafmuch as by turning the ftream
of Government out of its proper channel, it would have
utterly confounded the whole courfe of Natural and
Civil Right , which is the only Bafis or foundation of
Government in this world. And therefore feeing their
defign was of fo high a nature, as it aim'd at no lefs than
the extirpation of Law, and Government it felf, and of
the main Rights and Interefts of the People relating thereunto

unto; it is the lefs needfull to mention their intrenching
upon other Rights which are of an inferior confideration,
as in the matter of Tythes, and of Patronage and Prefentation of Minifters to Livings : Concerning which we
fhall only fay, that in this, as in all other things, nothing
of moderation would content them. It was propounded,
as the more fober and equitable way, That perfons of
eminent piety and fidelity might be appointed to judge of
fuch Minifters as fhould be prefented by Patrons : but
they would admit of no fuch regulation, running out into
the extreme, and quite voted away the whole Right of
Prefentation. And in the debate thereof they forbore not
to difcover the principle whereby they did it, judging all
men to be carnal and Antichriftian, that differed in opinion
from them.

III. As concerning the *Army*, this being the great
Impediment in the way of *their Monarchy*, they were
not without their defigns alfo upon it : which not being
to be contended with by any open attempt, they proceeded
towards it by other methods. For, when the neceffary
continuation of Affefsments came to be debated in the
Houfe, they laboured might and main (under fpecious
pretences) to have caft out the Bill, and fo at once to
have cut all the finews of the Army and their fubfiftence,
the only vifible fupport of the Nations fecurity : the confequence whereof would have been an expofing of the
Souldiery to Free-quarter and diforder, and thereby the
Country to rapine ; all fupplies muft have been cut off
likewife from the Navy, and our Affairs and Friends left
to fink or fwim in *Ireland* and *Scotland*; yea, and all this
at fuch a time of unufual danger and neceffity, when *Scotland* was unquiet, the Commonwealth engaged with Enemies abroad, and forced to an extraordinary Charge for
the maintenance of our Fleets at Sea, which are as the walls
and bulwarks of this Nation againft Invafions of Foreig-
ners. But the Bill of Affefsments being paft, and their intentions

tentions this way fruftrated,their next method was to have
alter'd the Government of the Army, and to have com-
mitted it to fuch hands as would have affifted them in
their intended Transformation. As a Preparative hereto,
all Courfes were taken to make the *Army* odious, the
Officers afperfed with the title of *Janifaries*, and men fet
up in Pulpits, whofe daily work was to caft dirt upon all
perfons in Truft and Power, in the Army and elfwhere,
by proclaiming them to be *Penfioners of Babylon*, and the
Government Antichriftian : which licentious Tongues
were not only encouraged herein by the prefence, but
affifted (many times) by the perfons of fome of their Patrons in the late Affembly. Nor did thefe men reft here:
but not being able to ferve their own wills and phant'fies
within the Houfe, fo eafily as they defired ; then they refolved to divide and feparate themfelves from the other
Members, who followed them not in their exceffes, and
to conftitute themfelves into a Power diftinct from them.
To this end, they led off divers well-meaning Gentlemen
of the Houfe along with them, to private Meetings of
their own appointment, upon pretence of feeking the
Lord by prayer for direction. But, to the great difhonor
of God, and prophanation of his holy Ordinances, the
ufe that was made of thofe Meetings by the Contrivers of
them, was, only for the better carrying on of things that
they had beforehand refolved to act. And in order thereto, they took liberty to arraign and condemn the perfons
and proceedings of their fellow-Members, and provoked
others to Remonftrate and Proteft againft them ; faying,
That if the Houfe then fitting fhould fend for them, they
ought not to obey them : Devifing alfo at the fame Meetings, which way to prepoffefs all the gather'd Churches
in *England* by Letters, and with Reports of their own to
fcandalize the Government in the opinion of our Brethren
in thofe Churches, whofe Liberties we tender as our own
in the Lord, and for whofe fatisfaction this Difcourfe is
chiefly intended ; endeavouring thereby to lead afide the
Godly

Godly of the Land into miftakes and offences. And when they could not obtain a generall confent to write unto the Churches, becaufe many of the Meeting perceived the evil of this bufinefs, it was left to every mans difcretion to write as he fhould fee caufe and occafion. Befides all this, direction was given at a Meeting, to pull down fome of the great Officers, and put others in their places ; thereby to create fuch difcontents and emulations among the Souldiery, as would probably have divided and embrued them in each others blood, and expofed them and the whole Nation for a prey to the common Enemy.

Things being at this pafs, and the Houfe (through thefe Proceedings) perfectly disjointed , and the two Parties wound up to fuch a height of animofity, that they were as much divided, as if they had been people of two diftinct Nations, mutually contending for each others Rights, it was in vain to look for a Settlement of this Nation from them thus conftituted ; but on the contrary, nothing elfe could be expected, but that the Commonwealth fhould fink under their hands, and the great Caufe hitherto fo happily upheld and maintained,be for ever loft, through their prepofterous management of thofe Affairs wherewith they had been trufted. And therefore the major part of that Affembly being convinced, that they could fit no longer, without incurring the guilt of that deftruction which was coming on the whole Land, did upon the 12. day of *December* 1653. by fubfcribing their Names to an Inftrument in writing, refign up their Powers and Authorities to his now *Highnefs* (then Captain-General of all the Forces of this Commonwealth) in thefe following words:

Upon

Decemb. 12. 1653.

UPon a *Motion this day made in the House, that the fitting of this Parlament any longer as now Conftituted, will not be for the good of the Commonwealth; and that therefore it was requifite to deliver up unto the* Lord General Cromwell, *the Powers which they received from Him, Thefe Members whofe names are underwritten, have and doe hereby refigne their faid Powers to his Excellencie.*

Which being done, and thereby all Power of Govern-ment devolved upon the General, as Head of the Army, it was neceffary to take fpeedy confideration, in what Form to difpofe the Government. To have continued it in a Military way, had been dangerous; and inconfiftent with the Freedom of the People, and by confequence to have inthroned Power and Force above Law, and left both the inftituting and executing of Law to the arbitrary difcretion of the Souldier, who being girt with both Swords of War and Civil Juftice, would be apt to miftake and draw the one, inftead of the other, to execute his own will in place of Law, without check or controll, having all force at his own difpofition; which muft have intro-duced very great inconveniences.

To have returned back again to *Reprefentatives,* as the Parlament had propounded in their *Biennial Bill,* and fo to have governed thefe Nations by Parlaments alwayes fitting, not only clear reafon, but experience evinceth, that neither Safety nor Liberty could be expected therein. Parlaments always fitting are no more agreeable to the temper of this People, than it is to a natural Body to take always Phyfick inftead of Food. For, the prime end of the Parliamentary conftitution is to make Laws, and redrefs grievances. Now it cannot in reafon be imagined, that becaufe the great Body of the People may fometimes a- bound with ill humors and diftempers, therefore it fhould be perpetually under the hands of it's Phyficians : This may fooner kill than cure. The ordinary preventive phy- fick in a State againft growing maladies, is execution and adminiftration of Law and Juftice, which muft be left to its Officers ; but Legiflation or the power of Law-making is then properly exercifed, when they are grown to a height, & have need of ftrong purgation; which if conftantly ufed, vitiates the Complexion, enervates the natural vigor, and fortifies the difeafe by a more abundant acceffion of perni- cious humors. What Commonwealth that hath but a face of civility, can be fuppofed to have People of fo forlorne a difpofition at all times, and things fo continually out of order, that it will require a perpetual application of new Laws for remedy ? which if admitted, would in a fhort time require fome Ages to read over innumerable Statutes, and reduce the bufinefs of Law to as bad condition, as it was in the *Roman* Empire before the dayes of *Juftinian*, when by long tract of time the Laws were fwoln into fo prodigious a heap of untractable volumes, that the Law- profeffors themfelves were oppreffed under the weight of them, as well as the People. And as to what concerns us here in *England*, we were fairly coming on to the fame pafs ; fo many Laws having been ordained the laft Parlia- ment, that our *Gentlemen of the Robe* know very well what ado there is to reconcile one Law and Ordinance with another, how incongruous they are in refpect of themfelves, and in reference to many antient Laws which immediately concern the Liberty of the People. So that

D   had

had they been left to their own will, to have sate Ordaining as long as they list, a few years more would have mounted the Statute-book above the reach of a Student's purse, and advanced it to the size of an antient *Livy*, which was held sufficient of it self to set out a whole Library; by which means the Sense of Law could never have been extricated out of endless Intanglements, but being lost in the Labyrinth of its own Bulk, it must have proved a miserable vexation both to Lawyer and Client. These would have been the effects of ever-sitting Parliaments, in point of Law-making. But as to an assuming to themselves also a distribution of Law and Justice, it is a thing not to be once named among a free People, whose security lies in having an easie open way of Appeal, in case of wrong done by Justicers; which can very rarely, or never be had against the Injury of so supreme a Court as a Parlament, it being the highest. But admit they were accountable ever to the succeeding Parlament, yet (when all is done) it would be a hard matter to question so great a Body, a course very ill-beseeming the dignity of Parlaments; and as difficult a point to pick out Offenders, a way too much reflecting upon the liberty of Parlament, which lies in a freedom of Debate; and this every man will challenge, and say he did but speak his Judgment, if any one should be called to account for promoting an unjust Determination. Nay, put case, that particular Offenders of this kind could be singled out of the House, yet for all this, the people would be very desperately to seek of remedies against their arbitrary Dictates, because those great moliminous Bodies of Parlaments are but slow in motion, and attendance will quickly exhaust a good purse and patience, before any thing can be done; the truth of all which we well knew by experience, through the continued Session of the late Parlament. Where Law is dispensed, there should upon occasion of injury be a ready passage to redress against the Dispensers, or else as good be without any Law at all: But this cannot be expected.

pected from continual Parlaments, and therefore as they were never intended for executioners of Law (it being the peculiar Task of inferior Courts) and as there is no need, but very great inconvenience that they should be busied still in framing Laws, which is their principal work; so it must of necessity be granted, that their perpetuated sitting in the Nation, would have been unnecessary, dangerous, and its most deplorable Grievance.

Lastly, to have called again particular persons to the Supreme Government, in the way last taken by erecting the late Assembly, the evil thereof was too notorious and fresh in memory, and therefore dangerous to venture a splitting upon that Rock again, which had been but newly escaped. We, and all the People, had need beware of that mistaken principle, which had like to have devoured the common Interest of our Nation. For, we cannot yet but admire at those mens open and violent avowing this Point of State-heresie; *That godly persons, though of small understanding, and little ability of mind in publick Affairs, are more fit for Government than men of great knowledg and wisdom, if endued only with natural Parts, and moral vertues*; whereupon they are too apt to think, that none ought to be intrusted in Government but godly persons, or such as are Saints by calling, who shall have immediate assistance from God suitable to their work. But alas, our late experience hath sufficiently taught us, that God works not now in any such extraordinary way, but hath left the world to be ordered by the moral improvement of natural Endowments and Faculties. The businefs of Government is not conversant about the inward graces and Qualifications of men, as men of Faith and justified persons, but is wholly terminated in works of the outward man; It being purposedly ordained for a terror to evil doers, and the praise or encouragement of them that doe well, according to the light of nature, and dictates of the natural Conscience; which summs up the main duty of a

D 2   Chri-

Chriſtian Magiſtrate, who ought to|keep himſelf within
theſe Bounds. And it is ſo far from the intent of Chriſt,
that his Sheep ſhould be folded within the Walls of a Supreme Authority, that he plainly told his Diſciples, and us
in them , that *his Kingdom is not of this world* ; whereby
he totally diſcountenanceth that worn *Tenet*, long ſince
exploded, but now revived by theſe men, *That temporal
Power and Authority is and ought to be founded in grace.* A
thing ſo little minded by *Paul*,and ſo far from the thoughts
of the reſt of the Apoſtles and Penmen of the New Teſta-
ment, that men as Saints might claim a Right and Title
to become Governors and Princes, that they are bid rather to arm themſelves with patience for Tribulation and
perſecution, as their portion in this world, and to think
rather of praying for Kings and Magiſtrates, counting it
ſufficient if by prayer they might obtain ſo much favour
under them, as to live a quiet and peaceable life. The
knowledg of God in Chriſt was never given forth to govern the world, but for more high and noble ends; as to
live in communion with God ; to bridle and quench a
mans luſts and diſorderly affections, and to ſubject the
whole inward man to the Rules of another, even a ſpiri-
tual Kingdom. It is a thing indeed to be wiſhed, that
Governors might alwaies be endued with the grace and the
knowledg of God in Chriſt. added to thoſe great gifts of
moral vertue, Wiſdom and Prudence, becauſe it puts a
luſtre upon them all, and makes the Government very
beautifull; but Grace (though moſtly accompanied with
ſome meaſure of thoſe gifts) doth not neceſſarily quali-
fie gratious men alwaies with an excellency of diſcerning
in matters of a Civil nature ; for, we ſee many rich endowments of Underſtanding, Juſtice, Fortitude, patience, &c. in others (which many believers have not)
whereby they are fitted to rule men of ſeveral Tempers
and Paſſions, and to fore-ſee the Conſequents of things
by reaſon, and in a natural way ; which is the only means
ordained by God to rule the world, who hath left the
whole

(27)

whole Frame of nature here below to be regulated and disposed by the natural man. And therefore, whenever the Magistrate runs out of his sphere to act upon other grounds, or when men shall assume Magistracie to Themselves, upon any such ground (as aforesaid) beside that of naral and civil Right, they not only lay a Foundation (as we have lately seen) for imposing upon mens consciences, and severe persecution, but doe (as much as in them lies) proclaim war against all men besides their own Opinionists, cancelling the very Rights of Nature, together with all the Bonds of civil society.

Nor must it be forgotten here, what a Rock such men are ready to rush upon, who shall endeavour to twist the Spiritual and Civil Interest both in one, and so make the Church and State of the same extention, as they do who hold that none ought to be in Authority but Saints by calling; for, in this there is a recurring to the very Papall and Prelatick principle. Upon this notion the *Pope* first set up himself, and the Prelates after him, adding the Temporal Authority to the Spiritual, and so made the Kingdom of Christ to be of this world, as those poor deluded souls do, who lay the Foundation of their *Fifth Monarchy*, upon the same carnal Supposition.

Wherefore upon these, and divers other Considerations, it was agreed to come to some such solid and certain course of Settlement, as might hereafter barr up the way against those manifold inconveniences, which we have felt under other fleeting Forms, and reduce us (as near as may be, with most convenience) to our antient way of Government, by Supreme Magistrates and Parlaments.

And of this nature is the Form now established, and already made publick.

But to the end that this may be made clear and manifest, we shall in the next place discourse somwhat concerning it in generall, and then descend to particulars. In general,

generall, we fay ; that as this laft Change hath been made
upon the fame grounds of reafon and equity, that neceffi-
tated all foregoing Changes in the outward Forms, and
was admitted of abfolute neceffi:y to fave a finking Nation out of the gulf of mifery and confufion, caufed by the
changeable Counfels and corrupt Interefts of other men,
who violated their Principles, and brake the Truft com-
mitted to them : So none of thofe former Alterations did
fo truly make good, or fo fully provide for the fecurity
of thofe great ends of Religion and Liberty, which were
as the blood and fpirits running through every vein of the
Parlament and Armies Declarations ; fo that though the
Commonwealth may now appear with a new face in the
outward Form, yet it remains ftill the fame in Subftance,
and is of a better complexion and conftitution then heretofore.

If we take a furvey of the whole together, we find the
Foundation of this Government laid in the People. Who
hath the power of altering old Laws, or making new ?
The people in Parlament ; without them nothing of this
nature can be done; they are to be governed only by fuch
Laws as they have chofen, or fhall chufe, and not to have
any impofed upon them. Then, who is to adminifter or
govern according to thofe Laws, and fee them put in execution? Not a perfon claiming an hereditary Right of
Soveraignty, or power over the Lives and Liberties of the
Nation by birth, allowing the People neither Right nor
Liberty, but what depends upon Royal grant and pleafure,
according to the tenor of that Prerogative challenged
heretofore by the Kings of *England* ; under whom, if
the Commonalty enjoyed any thing they might call their
own, it was not fo much to be efteemed a matter of Right,
as a Boon and effect of grace and favour. But the Government now is to be managed by a Perfon that is *elective*,
and that Election muft take its rife originally and virtually
from the People, as we fhall fully evince by and by, in particular, and fhew that all power both *Legiflative* and *Exe-*
cutive

(29)

native, doth flow from the Community; than which there cannot be a greater Evidence of publike Freedom.

Again, as this Person is not to exercise his Power by a Claim of Inheritance, or by vertue of any personal Right over and above the People; so it is a thing that he is to receive only by way of Trust, for their benefit and protection; and the power he is invested with, is not to make him great and glorious, otherwise then in order to the peace and advantage of those that are governed by him; whereas the Kings of this Nation pretended always, and maintained an Interest of their own, as they were Kings, distinct and superior to that of the People; which they called their own, as much as any particular man can call his houses or lands his own, wherein he hath a personal propriety. And as they did not hold themselves to have come in by the People, so neither did they conceive themselves obliged to govern, otherwise than for their own greatness: And although this Doctrine had been broached in some later Books and Prints, *that Kings were not for themselves, but for the People*; yet the Courtiers laughed in their sleeves at it, and we know it was esteemed heretical by the King and his Abettors. Nevertheless, how often, and in how many Declarations did the Parliament promise to make him a great and glorious King! and were content to have imbraced him in such a posture, in case he had hearken'd to their desires and demands! Whereas now the Terms of Glory and Greatness are omitted, and a ground-work is laid to make the Nation great and glorious, and our chief Magistrate so, no otherwise than may be conducing to the same end: So that it will appear the Government is sufficiently popular, the antient Liberties of *England* not only secured, but enlarged; and that although the *executive power* be placed in a single person, yet it stands upon a fairer account then in former times.

But.

But let us proceed now from Generals, to touch upon
some of the Particulars in the said Establishment; where
we find, that all the grand Acts of Soveraignty are either
immediately, or influentially, lodged in the People; not
only such as they claimed of right in the time of Kings,
but such as they never made any demand of.

I. The first and great Act of Soveraignty lies in the
Enacting, and the *altering or annulling of Laws*: which
is expresly provided to be in Parlament, and not otherwise
(save in some Cases, and that only untill the sitting of the
next Parlament, the reason whereof will appear by and
by;) And that the exercise of this Soveraign Power by
the People, may not by any means be avoided, sure provision is made likewise for a continual succession of Parlaments, it being done with such care and circumspection,
that the very circumstances of Provision are sufficient to
induce a perswasion, that the whole Establishment was
made with an aim at the publick Good, and not fitted for
the greatning of any particular Person. Which will farther appear by the following considerations.

1. Consider what care is taken for a succession of Parlaments. A Parlament is to be called every three years at
least, not leaving it at the pleasure of the chief Magistrate,
to do it or not to do it; but other persons, in case of his
Failer, are impower'd and required to issue forth Summons
without him; and that under the penalty of High-Trea-
son. Which Provision is agreeable in some sort to the
Triennial Bill, passed in the beginning of the last Parlament; and that at such a time, when the Nation was just-
ly sensible of their own Rights, and when they never
dreamt of a perpetual Parlament, nor of ever-sitting Parlaments, but desired only a convenient succession of those
Supreme Assemblies: And the same desire was often ite-
rated by the Army, in their Remonstrances and Declarations.

2. As

2. As to the Conftitution of Parliaments, it muft be obferved; That the Elections of perfons to fit in Parlament,
are diftributed in all Counties, with much more equality
and proportion than heretofore, according to what hath
been often declared, and propounded by the Army; as alfo
that full provifion is made to prevent Frauds in Elections,
and falfe Returns. And whereas the liberty of Electing is
reftrained only to fuch qualified perfons in each County,
whofe Eftates real or perfonal are valuable at the fumm of
200*l.* and they declared capable to elect Members to ferve
in Parlament; let it be confider'd, that the liberty of that
kind is drawn forth to a greater latitude, than in the daies
of Kings, when this Priviledg was exceedingly curtailed,
and communicated to thofe alone who were called *Free-hol-
ders,* as if they alone had been the men that ought to be
free : But now we conceive it is circumfcribed with fuch
prudence and caution, that it fits neither too ftreight nor
too loofe, to the Body of our Nation.

3. If we confider what perfons are to be elected, as well
as to elect, we fhall find a very Chriftian moderation ufed
therein. Care is taken that fuch perfons fhall not be chofen, who were in Arms againft the Parlament after the year
1641. unlefs they have been fince in the Parlaments Service,
and given fignal Teftimony of their good Affections thereto; by this means to prevent a bringing into the Supreme
Councils, thofe who have fo lately declared themfelves Enemies to the Caufe of God, and the true Intereft and Liberty of the People. But yet, there being hope, that fuch
men may in time, by living under a free Goverrment, drink
in better principles, that incapacity is determined after three
fucceeding Triennial Parlaments, except they be' *Roman-
Catholicks,* or fuch as have been Partakers with the barba-
rous and bloudy Rebels in *Ireland.* And to the end the
Qualifications to be obferved in Elections, may not become
void, a power is referved in the Council, to judge and ap-

E   prove

prove of such as shall be elected, before they sit; which Power is to last but for the three next Triennial Parlaments. And this doubtlefs is a much better means, to keep out of the Parlament, men dif-affected to the true Intereft of this Nation, and thereby fecure the Caufe fo long fought for, than that which a party in the late Parlament feemed to refolve upon, *viz.* to perpetuate themfelves for ever, and thereby keep out all others who might call them to an account, expofing the publick to hazard for their own private fecurity; as if the fafety of the Nation had been bound up in their particular perfons. So that as on the one hand, a fitting provifion is made, to preferve at prefent, the Power and Reins of Government, in the hands of thofe who have approved themfelves faithful in the late greatControverfie of Freedom and Liberty; fo on the other hand a juft and probable foundation is laid for extinguifhing all animofities, and putting into oblivion the memory of all thofe Feids and divifions contracted by Civil War; not only by admitting fuch to Government, who of enemies are already become faft friends, but by limiting a time, after which all diftinctions of this nature fhall be taken away, whereby through the blefling of God, the people may be harmonioufly difpofed to a lafting peace and fettlement. Which things were all particularly declared for by the Army, in the year 1647. upon the like grounds and reafons.

4. The Power of Parlaments is now fuch, that befide what former Parlaments had, for the examining and rectifying of exorbitances, calling Officers to account, &c. they may by the prefent Conftitution, make and repeal Laws of themfelves; by which means, that unlimited prerogative of a *Negative Voice,* the Darling of our Kings, a principal Flower of the Crown (as they accounted it) and a thing which the late King contended for, is now utterly abjured, and Provifion made, that in cafe the *Lord Protector* do not figne fuch Bills as fhall be prefented to him, within twenty daies, then afterward they fhall of courfe become Laws, as

full

full and effectual as if his Affent to them had bin obtained.

5. Laftly, Confider the continuance or duration of Parlaments, and it is Provided they fhall not be adjourned, prorogued, nor diffolved for five months fpace, without their own Confent; whereas, every one knows what was claimed, and alwaies exercifed by the Kings of *England*, to wit, a Power of diffolving Parlaments at their pleafure : But now the Liberty of Parlament is fetled in that particular, and fecured againft arbitrary and momentany Diffolution, it being impoffible for any to diffolve them, without their own Confents, before the appointed time : which being confider'd, together with their abfolute Power of Legiflation, in the manner here expreffed, we fuppofe there is nothing that can be thought of, for the Freedom and profperity of the People, which may not be effected by the Parlament, though the *Protector* fhould not give his Confent thereto.

1. But if in reference to this of Parlaments, it be Objected; That in the twenty fourth Article, a *Negative Voice* is placed in the *Protector*, as to whatever is contained in the faid Eftablifhment; and that in the twelfth Article, the Members Elected are by their Indentures, to be debarred from altering the Government, as it is declared to be in a fingle Perfon and a Parlament; and that thereby the Supreme Power is limited and reftrained in things moft natural to their Truft and Employment; It is anfwered, that though it be of neceffity, yet it were a thing to be wifhed, that Popular Confent might alwaies, and at all times, have the fole influence in the Inftitution of Governments; but when an Eftablifhment is once procured, after the many fhakings and Rents of civil Divifions, and Conteftings for Liberty, as here now in *England*, doubtlefs we have the greater reafon to value it, being purchafed at the price of our bloud, out of the claws of Tyranny; and we conceive it highly concerns us, to put in fome fure *Provifo*, to prevent a razing

of thofe Foundations of Freedom that have been but newly laid ; efpecially in fuch an Age as this, wherein men are
very apt to be rooting and ftriking at Fundamentals, and to
be running out of one Form into another ; and when it is
found alfo,what advantages the Common Enemy hath made
by our being in the condition of a *Floating Ifland*, through
neglect of any certain fettlement : Which being confidered, it was high time , fome Power fhould pafs a Decree upon the wavering humors of the People, and fay to this
Nation , as the Almighty himfelf faid once to the unruly
Sea ; *Here fhall be thy Bounds, hitherto fhalt thou come , and
no further*. Now this neceffary courfe for fettlement is no
more, than what was formerly agreed on by the Army , in
their great Remonftrance from St. *Albans* , upon the like
grounds of reafon, and upon fuch another occafion; wherein you may read the like *Provifo* , for tying up of Reprefentatives or Parliaments , to the Form of Eftablifhment
then intended. Nor can it be reputed otherwife than moft
reafonable and neceffary , after fo great Commotions and
Confufions by Civil War, as have been in this Nation; for
as much as in fuch Cafes, it is very rarely to be expected or
imagined, that a Government can be erected in the way of
Confent by the People ; and it being moft needfull , that
fome Government fhould be ; and of unavoidable neceffity, that fome fhould fet down the Rules of it ; and that
men fhould be tied to thofe Rules, unlefs we would alwaies
be altering and fhifting of Settlements, and fo live ever in
diftraction : Therefore furely, as this Reftriction to the
prefent Form, is (confidering the ftate and temper of Affairs) moft undeniably neceffary, as the only courfe to keep
us from wandring any more in the Maze of our own Con-
tentions ; fo it is no new thing in the world , nor without
example from the Army it felf, even at that time , when
they were by fome men reputed moft pure , and fincerely
devoted to the Principles of Freedom.

2. Again,

2. Again, it may perhaps in the second place be objected, That whereas twenty dayes time are allowed to the *Lord Protector* to deliberate upon such Bills as shall be presented to him for his consent by the Parlament, therefore this seems to intrench upon the wisdom of Parlament (which is the wisdom of the whole Nation) as if they would not be well advised of such Bills as shall be intended for Laws. But for Answer, we must have recourse to the wisdom of our Anceftors touching this Particular, who doubtlefs might think themselves as wise in worldly matters, as succeeding Parlaments may be ; yet we find they used great deliberation in paffing all Laws. And thus much was fignified to us by the reading a Bill so many times, the Committing, and the Ingroffing it, with divers other Ceremonies used; which were to no other end but to stave off the hasty and precipitate nature of man from falling upon the rocks of any rash Conclusions, in matters of so high importance : And therefore upon this account it was, that they thought meet to allow the Supreme Magistrate likewise a time of deliberation, that when he paffed his Affent, he might do it as a Man, upon grounds of proper Judgment and Reafon; it being prefumed, that He being in all things affifted by a Councel, might perhaps have some Reafons to offer, not unworthy of confideration, conducing to the regulation and amendment of Particulars in things prefented to him. Hence it was that of old, when the King thought it needfull to deliberate upon matters of that nature, his Anfwer was, *Le Roy l'avifera*, that is, *the King will advife* : And this was pleaded to him by the late Parlament, as the antient Prerogative of the fupreme Magiftrate, in oppofition to his Plea for a *Negative voice*. And therefore, feeing this limited time of deliberation can no more derogate from the wisdom of Parlaments hereafter, than it was thought to do in elder time ; and whereas the Reafon holds now as ftrong as ever(if not more) for avoiding heady determinations in grand Affairs,

whereof

whereof the laſt Parlament gave us ſad experience (Laws having been made and unmade in an inſtant, and like imperfect Embrio's, ſtill-born, or elſe ſtrangled as ſoon as brought into the world) We muſt needs therefore be of opinion, that the *twenty dayes time* of deliberation reſerved unto the *Lord 'Protector* upon the like occaſions, cannot be any prejudice to the wiſdom of Parlament, but rather tends very much every way to the advantage of them and the Nation.

3. If it be in the third place objected, that the Limitation of the ſitting of Parlaments to the time of five months, is an impoſing upon them ; Wee would fain reaſon out the matter with ſuch men, and deſire them to conſider, that unleſs we would have Parlaments ſit ever, there muſt needs be an intimation of ſome certain time for them to riſe, and wherein it may be required of them ; for otherwiſe there is a dore left open for a perpetuation of particular perſons in ſoveraign power : And how unapt men are of their own accord to part with ſuch power, when they have got it once into their hands, how apt they are to corrupt like ſtanding Pools, and contract an arbitrary diſtemper in execution of Law, and what miſerable inconveniences muſt follow thereupon, we, and all the people of the Land can tell by too ſad experience. We would not ſeem hereby to bring an ill Report upon Parlaments, nor undervalue them to the world, becauſe of ſome miſcarriages of the laſt, knowing they are the beſt and moſt proper Phyſick to cure the diſeaſes of the Nation ; and therefore it was well ſaid of the *Obſervator* (a man much for Parlaments at the beginning of the War, and one whoſe wiritings were highly prized of the Parlament) *that Parlamentary government ſhould be uſed like Phyſick, by the intermiſſion of due ſpaces of Time, and not as Diet* ; otherwiſe, by too long uſe it will corrupt and deſtroy, inſtead of curing the Body. So that we ſee there is a neceſſity of having Intervals, or times when Parlaments are not ſitting. Now conſider

fider alfo, the great fault of the Kingly government in this
refpect was, that feeing no convenient time of fitting was
fixed as a Boundary, to keep off an overflowing will and
prerogative from intruding upon Parlaments, and break-
ing in upon them by violence, Kings took upon them to
diffolve them at pleafure in a moment, yea many times as
foon as they were met, and before the leaft redrefs had of
the Peoples grievances : And therefore the prudence of
the prefent Government hath fo well temper'd all Ingredi-
ents in the conftitution of Parlaments, and provided fo far,
that, as Phyfick, they may have a certain due time allotted
for operation (which before they had not) and for five
moneths fpace not be adjourned , prorogued, nor diffolved without their own confent. Wherein feeing there
is a fure provifion made againft an immediate arbitrary
Diffolution, with an implicite Referve, and a clear intimation that they may fit much longer, and as long as the
neceffities of the Nation fhall require ; and feeing when
Parlaments fhall have had their courfes a while, five moneths
fpace will be found a fair time for redrefs of grievances, and
fupplying other publike neceffities that may happen in the
fhort Intervals (wherein alfo a new Parlament may be
called, out of the ufual courfe, if there fhall be extraordinary occafion ;) feeing alfo that the way of Government
in free Nations is not to be accommodated unto Schemes
of Freedom which lie in melancholy contemplation, but
muft be fuited to that Form which lies faireft for practical
convenience, and avoiding Inconveniences, for the eafe
and fafety of the People ; and laftly, feeing it is a far lefs
inconvenience, that Parlaments fhould be limited in time,
rather then fit as long as they pleafe, and there can be
no Inconvenience here where a competent time is fixed,
but it is (all things confider'd) a very great Convenience : Therefore, fetting one thing againft another, we conceive, there can be no detriment accruing unto Parlaments
by fuch a limitation of time, and conferring all thefe things
together, we fuppofe lefs danger to be feared from a Power

er of Diffolution thus qualified, and but tacitly referved in
one perfon, and that perfon accountable for abufe of fuch
Power, than that Parlaments (who are, we fee, no more
priviledg'd from error than *Popes* and *general Councils*)
fhould be left to perpetuate themfelves as they pleafe, and
confequently to do what they pleafe, being, as long as they
keep their Seats, unaccountable perfons. The fumm of all
then that hath been faid, amounts to this; That there is
unqueftionably as great a neceffity, there fhould be fome
fet-time for the diffolution, as for the calling of Parlaments.
And truly, fo much was implied in all the Declarations of
the Parlament, before they thought of perpetuating themfelves. And if you remember, in the year 1647. the like
time of limitation (though not the very fame) was intended by the *Propofals* of the Army; upon the expiration
whereof each Parlament was to have diffolved of *courfe*, *if
not otherwife diffolved fooner*.

Having thus concluded that part of our Difcourfe,
which relates to the Succeffion and Conftitution of Parlaments in all Particulars, and made it evident therein,
that the Firft and greateft Act of Soveraignty, which
confifts in the Point of *Law-making*, is referved entire
in Parlament; and having alfo removed out of the way
the moft materiall Objections, we fhall now proceed to
the fecond.

II A fecond grand Act of Soveraignty is the dif-
pofall of the *Militia*; concerning which it cannot but
be remembred, that the King chalenged an abfolute
power, in and over it, to himfelf, as his fole Right,
exclufive and independent of the Parliament at all times.
The Parliament, they denyed this, and affirmed, that
his power over it was but by way of ordinary Truft;
and that in times of extraordinary danger and neceffity,
when he neglected to perform that Truft, then Themfelves were to fecure the *Militia*, and put it in execution,
as being more immediatly intrufted on the behalf of the
People:

People : And it muſt be remembred withall , that the utmoſt of the Parlament's demand of the *Militia* was but for a time, and the onely ground of their Demand was upon an unuſuall occaſion. But now, that Claim of the King (upon which he founded the main of his Quarrel) is wholly waved. and its exprefly declared ; that the *Lord Protector* ſhall diſpoſe and order the *Militia* or Forces both by Sea and Land, while the Parlament ſits, onely by Conſent of Parlament, and in the Intervals of Parliament, with the advice and conſent of the major part of the Councill. So that you ſee, the People's Parlamentary Intereſt in the great buſineſs of the *Militia*, is avowed and confirmed. And in caſe any thing ſhall be done hereafter concerning it, in the Intervals, by the Council, that may be matter of miſcarriage, there is a way of rectification and remedy left open, in the ſucceeding Parlament.

III. A third Prerogative of Soveraignty is the *making of Warr and Peace*; and that by the conſtitution of this Government, is not only to be manag'd with the Advice and conſent of the Council, but is communicated alſo to Parlaments : For, in caſe of future Warr with any Forein State, a Parlament ſhall be forthwith ſummoned to adviſe with concerning the ſame. Which is a Priviledg, that never was demanded by the Parlament in their *Nineteen Propoſitions* (ſuppoſed the higheſt demands) that were made at firſt to the King, nor in any of their firſt Declarations, but alwaies admitted to be in the King.

IV. A fourth Act of Soveraignty is the *Impoſing of Taxes and Payments*; and this is wholly reſerved to Parlaments; it being fit, that thoſe only who are in immediate Truſt from the People, ſhould have the Command of their Purſes. And whereas in the thirtieth Article of Government, there is a Clauſe reſerving a temporary Power in the

F   *Lord*

Lord Protector, with the Consent of the Council , to raise
money for preventing the disorders and dangers which may
otherwise fall out ; it must be observed , that as this is no
more but what is of pure necessity, and to continue only till
the sitting of the first Parlament ; so it is much less than
what was propounded by the Army in the year 1647. when
the like power was desired might be given to a Council or
Committee, in the Intervals of Parlament.

V. The Fifth Point of Soveraign Power is, the *Highest
and last Appeal* , which is retained likewise in Parlament.

VI. The Sixth and last Point of Soveraignty is, the *Power of
Creating and disposing Magistrates and Officers*;which we are
bold to say,from the highest to the lowest,is stil placed either
expresly , or implicitly and ultimately in the hands of the
People in Parlament, as we shall make evident anon, when
we come to treat of the several Articles relating unto
that Particular , the consideration whereof will very fitly
fall in at the close of this Discourse , as its more convenient
place. In the mean time , seeing these Acts of Soveraignty are all comprehended within the Walls of a Parlament,
we must undeniably conclude, that as this Government now
established , answers all the Primitive Demands that were
made by the Parlament to the late King , as the means to
make this a florishing Nation ; so it exceeds them in many
particulars,for preservation of theFreedom,commonInterest,
and safety of the people. Thus far then , we suppose it appears, that we stand firm to our Principles.

But to proceed ; The next thing we are to take notice
of in this Government, is, That it fully answers likewise the
main ends of the Parlament and Army, in reference to matters of *Religion* ; wherein the Rights and Liberties of the
People are as duely fenced and provided for , as in all the
principal Points of Civil Interest and Freedom. For it may
be

be remembred, that the great care of the Parlament was (excluding ever licentious and blasphemous Opinions and Practises) to make a Christian provision for the Liberty of tender Consciences; They made it their business to protect and countenance Religious men and Godliness in the power of it, to give freedom and enlargement to the Gospel (for the increasing and spreading of light in this darksom world) and thereupon to remove all superstitious or corrupted Forms that were opposite thereto : which things were indeed the proper Subject of that religious Reformation intended by them, and which hath been often declared for by the Army. In conformity to which blessed and most Christian design, we suppose a special regard is now had to all the Interests of Gods people, with *the Maintenance of the Ministry, the Confutation of Error and Heresie, the Extirpation of Popery, Prelacy, and whatsoever is contrary to Godliness and sound Doctrine*; as you may see in the 35. 36. 37. and 38. Articles of Government. And whereas in the 36. and 37. Articles it is intimated or implied, that there is a Publick profession intended to be held forth by the Magistrate, and that the Profession so held forth shall extend both to Doctrine, and Worship or Discipline; whereupon some persons do object, that this is contrary to the Principles formerly owned by the *Army*: We return this answer : That whatever the private Judgments and opinions of many particular persons in the Army may heretofore have been concerning this matter, yet the Body of the Army never declared themselves either against the Magistrates power in matters of Religion, or that the Magistrate might not hold forth a publick Profession of Doctrine and Discipline ; but we find the quite contrary clearly implied and expressed in their *Declarations* and *Proposals*. For, in their *Proposals* they found fault with nothing of that nature, but moved only for the taking away of all *Coercive power*, Authority and Jurisdiction of all Ecclesiastical Officers whatsoever, extending to civil penalties upon any; and for the repealing of all Acts imposing penalties for not coming to

Church,

Church, or for meetings elfwhere, &c. And in that Declaration of *June* 14. 1647. (which may ferve once for all) they clearly difclaimed and difavow'd any defign to overthrow all Church-government; only defired, that according to the Parlaments Declarations (promifing a provifion for tender Confciences) there might fome effectual courfe be taken anfwerable to the intent thereof, and that fuch who upon confcientious grounds fhould differ from the eftablifhed Forms,might not (for that) be debarred from the Common Rights, Liberties, or Benefits belonging equally to All, as men and members of the Commonwealth, while they live foberly, honeftly, and inoffenfively towards others, and peacefully and faithfully towards the State, Which Judgment and Refolution of the Army at that time (which fome men are pleafed to call and account the time of their Virgin-innocence and purity) exactly fquares with the Intent and Frame of the prefent Government, in things of Religion, as it is fet forth in thefe Articles. And therefore, feeing it never was any Principle of the Army, that the Magiftrate fhould be deprived of that power, whereby he is principally inabled to fulfill the moft noble end of his Magiftracie (and in comparifon whereof all other Ends are of an inferior value;) And feeing it is a duty incumbent upon the Magiftrate, to provide for the Civil peace, and to prevent fore-feen evils and inconveniences growing upon the Commonwealth, tending to Confufion; Obferving alfo what advantages have been made by the Popifh party both at home and abroad, through our want of fome Settlement in Religious matters, and what occafions have thereby been given to fubtile heads and carnal minds to difplay innumerable Parties and Factions under the banner of Religion, fpreading abroad moft blafphemous Opinions in defiance even of the holy Scriptures, and of God the *Father, Son,* and *Spirit*, to the difhonour and fcandal of our Chriftian profeffion ; And finally, it being manifeft, that in thefe things men do make fhipwrack of Faith and a good Confcience, for worldly ends and advantages which

they

they propound unto themselves, not only to the apparent hazard, vexation, and disquiet of the Commonwealth, but (as much as in them lies) to the licentious subverting of all Order and Government; therefore we conceive it is high time for our Governours to lay a healing hand to these mortal wounds and breaches, by holding forth the Truths of Christ to the Nation in some solid Establishment, and not quite to lay aside or let loose the golden reins of Discipline & Government in the Church; but yet to order them in such a way that they may not tie up all mens Consciences, who profess Truth in sobriety, to any one particular Form, nor be laid as snares and chains upon conscientious and zealous men (as it was wont to be in the dayes of Popery and Prelacy;) the summ of all that is intended by way of Coercion, being only to restrain such as shall abuse their Liberty to the Civil injury of others, and to the actual disturbance of the publick Peace, or such as under the profession of Christ hold forth and practise Licentiousness.

The next considerable in the Government is, the way of maintenance for the Forces both by Sea and Land, and this is to be done by a constant yearly Revenue. The set-number of Land-Forces to be kept up, is 10000 Horse and Dragroons, and 20000 Foot, which doubtless is but a competent number for the defence of three such Nations, as *England*, *Scotland*, and *Ireland*, and they are to be maintained with part of that Revenue; the rest is to be expended in a convenient number of Ships for the Guard of the Seas: And in case there shall not be cause hereafter to keep up so great a Defence at Sea and Land, then the money saved thereby, is to remain *in Banco* for the Publick Service, and be imployed by consent of Parlament; which, questionless, being seriously ponder'd, is a most excellent Provision, and such as will not only give us credit and esteem among our Friends abroad, but strike Terror into our Enemies, when they see the Government continually fortified with the sinews of Warr, by a constant Revenue for that purpose,

and

and with this grand advantage alfo of a publick Bank or
Treafury upon all occafions. And though the great benefit and convenience of this cannot be feen and felt, till God
pleafe to free us from the prefent chargeable Occafions; yet
when thefe neceffities fhall (through his bleffing) be over,
and an oportunity given, that the Land-Forces (which in
Field and Garifon within the Three Nations are now at leaft
80000 in number) may be reduced to the fetled proportion, and the Nation begin to enjoy fome meafure of Peace
and Settlement, it will be found a great eafe unto the generality, that the Commonwealth fhall (as it will ordinarily)
by this means be inabled to defend it felf, offend enemies,
and affift its Allies and Confederates upon a Publick Stock,
without impofing any Taxes or Payments extraordinary upon the People. And furely it will be farr lefs burthen for
the Commonalty to contribute thus in fmall Parcels yearly,
towards the publick Bank and Revenue, than to be affeffed
at great fums, whenfoever the Government fhall have neceffity to raife monies upon great occafions, to wage Warr,
or for the defence of thefe Nations.

Then as for the Two hundred Thoufand pounds *per annum*, which is to be fetled over and above, it is not for the
fupport of the *Protector*, or to be taken for the private ufe
of any particular perfon or perfons whatfoever, but to be
employed (as may be feen in the 27 Article) in defraying
the Charges for Adminiftration of Juftice, and other Expences of the Government: *viz.* for paying the Salaries
of Judges, and other Officers belonging to Courts of
Judicature, the neceffary expences for carrying on the Publick bufinefs in all the three Nations, the entertaining Ambaffadors here, the fending out Ambaffadors and Agents,
&c. into Forein Parts, the relieving of maimed Soldiers,
and many like chargeable ufes. All which confidered, it
will be found (we fear) too fmall a fumm for fuch a Work;
efpecially feeing the fingle expences of the late *Council of
State*

State amounted to above one hundred Thoufand pound *per annum.*

The laſt and great point of Soveraignty and concernment to the fafety and benefit of a Commonwealth (which we touched a little before) is the *Electing and diſpoſing of it's own Magiſtrates,* or the great Officers of State ; and we find in the 34. Article, that the *Chancelor, Keeper or Commiſſioners of the Great Seal,* the *Treaſurer, Admirall , Chief Governors* of *Ireland* and *Scotland,* and the *Chief Juſtices* of both the Benches, are to be choſen only by approbation of Parlament; which anſwers fully to former deſires of the Parlament and Army.   And as to what concerns the *Councill,* though the Election of them be not directly and immediately, yet virtually and ultimately it is in the People in Parlament , and muſt flow indeed originally from Them in time to come.   For, upon the death or removal of any Member of the Council , the Parlament are to nominate fix perſons of ability, integrity, and fearing God, out of which the Major part of the Council ſhall elect two, and preſent them to the *Lord Protector,* of which he ſhall elect one, to ſupply the vacancy; So that if an unworthy perſon be at any time choſen , it muſt be the Parlaments fault , who have the power of making the firſt choice , and conſequently of limiting both the *Lord Protector* and the Council in the main; as alſo of preventing any corruption , which either of them might otherwiſe be guilty of in this Particular.   Moreover, in caſe any Member of the Councill ſhall prove corrupt in his Truſt, then ſeven Members of Parlament being joyned with fix of the Council, are to judge of the buſineſs, by which means, whatſoever the caſe be , the Parlament hath the caſting Voice , and greateſt Vote in the Judgment. Thus the courſe of Election is ſtated for the time to come.

But as for the *preſent Councill,* and the election of them
in

in the way it hath been; It muſt be remembred, that we were in the beginning of a new Government, neceſſitated to create a little World out of *Chaos*, and bring Form out of Confuſion; ſo that there was an abſolute neceſſity, that ſome who are known to be perſons of Integrity, and firm for the preſent Settlement, ſhould at the ſame inſtant be taken in, to carry on the work: which can be no ground of juſt exception, eſpecially ſeeing for the future, Elections ſhall run in the appointed channel, where their ſtreams are to flow from the People, as their original-Fountain. Yea, the high Office of *Protectorſhip* it ſelf is to be derived alſo from hence; and as in time it will appear, that the People in Parlament have the main choice of the Council, ſo they will likewiſe be Chuſers of the *Lord Protector*: For, it being left to the Council to chuſe Him, and they hereafter coming to be choſen and truſted by the Parlament, it cannot otherwiſe be conceived, but that the Choice of Him takes its riſe mediately from the People in Parlament: becauſe as whatſoever a Parlament doth, is ſaid and taken in a political ſenſe to be the Peoples act, becauſe they are choſen and truſted by the People; ſo in like manner, and upon the ſame political account, when the Council comes to be choſen by Parlaments, as is before expreſſed, then the Act of the Council in chuſing the *Lord Protector*, muſt by a parity of Reaſon be reputed the Act of the People in Parlament. And ſo you ſee, in effects mediately or immediately, the election of all Magiſtrates (both high and low) are, or will at length, by this Conſtitution of Government, be in the hands of the People.

Laſtly, as to what concerns the Office of *Lord Protector*, it is to be obſerved, that no man is to be admitted to that Dignity upon the Intereſt of Himſelf or Family, but meerly upon the account of his Fitneſs for Government; it muſt paſs, not by Inheritance, but Election. And certainly, it is a great advantage to a Nation, that the coming in and continuance of their Governour depends only upon his own
goodneſs,

goodnefs, and the good will of the People, as it is in an *Elective Prince*, who ftanding upon Terms of good behaviour, will be continually employed for the benefit and defence of the Community. And therefore, if it fhall pleafe the Lord to blefs this Commonwealth (as we truft he will) fucceffively, with a choice of godly perfons into that high Office, it is eafily fore-feen, what an advantage it will be to thefe three Nations, to have their whole ftrength and Force combined thus under one head, for the fafety of all; this Form being (without queftion) the fitteft and moft convenient for the Magiftrate to put things on, and in quick execution (as his proper work) for the publick good; as alfo what a comfort it will be to all the godly in the *Proteftant Churches* abroad, who may have ground to expect fome more fure and certain Protection from *England* than heretofore; which as it is the greateft Body, being united with *Scotland*, fo it will prove (we hope) the grand Bulwark of the *Reformed Religion.*

Moreover, as touching the Perfon, whom the Lord hath now advanced and fet over us to be our Supreme Magiftrate, We fhall not fay much, becaufe he feeks not the praife of men; only we believe even the enemies will confefs, that he is every way worthy to Rule, whom God hath been pleafed to ufe as his Inftrument in that Glorious Work of Redeeming the Liberties of his People: For, we are bold to fay (weighing all circumftances together) that this Nation was never really Free, nor in a way of enjoying its Freedom fo fully as now; fo that there wants nothing but a cordial Clofe with the Government, to deftroy all hopes of the common Enemy, and compleat our happinefs. But if men fhall yet proceed to lengthen their own burthens, by hankering after that Family which God hath caft out before us, or by an unnatural feeking to imbroil their Country again in bloud and mifery, for the fake of that accurfed Intereft, as we are loth to fufpect fuch a thing, and can

G   hardly

hardly imagin that any should be so forlorn and desperate after so fair a Compolure : So we think it necessary to reclaim such persons, if any there be inclined that way, by laying down these few Considerations concerning that Person and Family which pretends to the Government of these Nations.

1. It is a Family that hath worn the Marks and Badges of Gods high displeasure for almost these hundred years : the weight of which vengeance hath fallen upon, and hitherto sunk all their Partakers ; the particulars whereof being in every mans view, and many of them fresh in observation, we shall not here enumerate.

2. If we reflect upon the Person of the *young Pretender*, he is by bloud almost a stranger to this Nation, being by the Mother a *French-man*, and now unquestionably such by his education in that Court, where he hath alwaies before his eyes that patern of absolute Power which bewitched his Father. Besides, he is a man of Bloud, having involved himself in the guilt of all that innocent Bloud which was spilt by his Father, and hath added more to it since, to fill up the measure of that Transgreffion.

3. His Religion (if any) is at best, you know, but a devotion to Prelacy (which was bequeathed to him in Legacy) having forfeited his Oaths to the *Scotish* Nation, and all his other Pretences of Religion there, before ever he left the Country. What Profeffion he owns in *France*, is hardly visible, but his Mothers Instructions, the urgency of his necessities disposing him to imbrace any thing, his dependence upon forein Papists, his frequent known applications and promises to the *Pope*, by special Agents employed to *Rome* for that purpose, and to the *Emperor*, his Alliance to, and Combination
tion

(49)

tion with Popish Princes, being put all together in the balance, is ground enough to believe him sufficiently affected, if not sworn to Popery. For, if he have any promise of assistance (as perhaps the Popish Party may now combine, seeing we are for a settlement of true Religion) it is to be presumed, those persons will not be forward to re-invest him here, unless they may together with him restore the *Roman-Catholick* Interest and Superstition.

4. The great and vast Debts that he hath in all this time contracted abroad (should he return hither) must all be discharged out of the purses of this exhausted Nation.

5. Consider the desperate Crew of forlorn Fugitives, Foreiners, and Papists, that he must bring along with him, which will like Locusts devour the whole Land before them; for, their insatiable Appetites must all be served, and great Rewards must be thought of for his Leaders and Followers; so that his Return will be so far from being a remedy or relief of Taxes, that the Nation it self will be too little for him and his.

6. The manifold Revenges and Cruelties that are to be expected : No mans life, no mans Estate can be secure : There will then be no distinction of Parties, and every small Compliance with what hath passed, every the least word shall be made guilt enough, and ground enough (if he please) for Death and Confiscation.

7. Lastly, an arbitrary uncontrolable will and power to put all these things in execution : For, if he ever get in by the sword, he becomes at the very instant as absolute as the *Grand Seignior*; and will then be fully inabled to accomplish what his Family had long projected, viz. the inthroning himself upon an Interest of meer will and power, against the common Interest of the People; by

G 2   which

which means our Lives and Liberties, our Wives and Children, our Estates and Fortunes, would all be exposed as a sacrifice to the boundles ambition and cruelty of a race of Tyrants; it would enervate the natural vigor and courage of the People, and exceedingly debase the honour of this free Nation.

Let us ruminate then a little in our hearts touching these things, and behold the great hopes and blessed benefits of Security and Freedom that we have, and may shortly enjoy under the Government, as it is now established. The Quarrel for hereafter is not between two Persons contesting both for a Crown; it is not the Interest or Grandeur of any single Person, or particular Family, that is contended for on our part: But if ever the Enemy should (for our sins) arise to the possibility of a future Contest, remember what it is he fights for, and what must be the wretched Consequents of his prevailing; remember also what we of this Nation are to stand for, the preservation of our Religion, our Liberties, and all that is dear and precious among men, which appear plainly to be imbarqued in the great Bottom of this present Establishment. If we falter, or be mis-led through phant'sie, or if that fail through our default, we are immediately swallowed up by Tyrannie, and have nothing left to do, but to put our mouths in the dust, and sit down in sorrow and silence for the glory of our Nation. Moreover, if on the other side any opposition of malecontent and refractory men should (which God forbid) arise at home here among our selves, the like Confusions will follow, the effect whereof must needs be a straining up the Pins of Power, to spoil the harmony of Government, and a constraining men, for necessary preservation, to fence themselves in such a manner as they never intended.

Having

Having therefore a fair and noble way of Administration provided, under which men may live in a plenary
enjoyment of their Liberty as Christians, and their Rights
as Men; we do not, we cannot in any measure doubt
(though we thus expostulate the matter with our Friends
and Countrymen, and lay open those great Inconveniences
and dangers before them) but that we shall find a ready
and cheerfull concurrence from all sober Persons; and
have ground chiefly to expect it from all the People
of God, though of different Judgments, seeing equal
Liberty is given to them all (without just offence to any)
and the principal care is for preserving true Religion, and
the countenance of its Professors. We, for our parts,
have done our duty, in declaring the grounds of our
Judgment, and know we have therein discharged a good
Conscience, in answer to all the Ends of our first Principles and Engagements, believing we shall find comfort
in it in the day of our Account : For, when we look back
upon what is done, we find nothing that stares in our faces;
and if there could have been imagined any better way of
Settlement, we should have imbraced it with the same
spirit of submission : But here we see, our Friends have
taken in the good of all the three sorts of Government,
and bound them all in one. If War be, here is the Unitive
vertue (but nothing else) of *Monarchy* to encounter it ;
and here is the admirable Counsel of *Aristocracie* to ma-
nage it : If Peace be, here is the industry and courage
of *Democracie* to improve it. And whereas in the present
Constitution, the *Legislative* and *Executive* Powers are
separated ; the former being vested in a constant succession of Parlaments elective by the People, the latter in
an elective *Lord Protector* and his Successors assisted by a
Council ; we conceive the State of this Commonwealth
is thereby reduced to so just a Temper, that the Ills either of successive Parlaments, furnished with power both
of executing and making Laws, or of a perpe ual Parlament, (which are Division, Faction, and Confusion)
being

(52)

being avoided on the one side, and the Inconveniences
of abfolute Lordly power on the other; the Frame of
Governmont appears fo well bounded on both fides, a-
gainſt Anarchie and Tyrannie, that we hope it may now
(through the bleſsing of God) prove a feaſonable
Mean (as for the better defending theſe Dominions a-
gainſt Enemies abroad, and promoting our Intereſts in
Forein parts, fo alfo) of Peace and Settlement to this
diſtracted Nation ; and be of a durable continuance to
fucceeding Ages, for the glory of the moſt high G O D,
the advancement of his Gofpel, the protection of his
People, and the benefit of Poſterity.

FINIS.